A Day in the Life of a...

Bus Driver

Carol Watson

W
FRANKLIN WATTS
LONDON • SYDNEY

Winston is a bus driver.
He starts his day by checking in
at the bus garage where he will
begin his route.

First Winston signs
on by swiping his
identity card through
a machine.
Then he opens up
his locker to get
out his equipment.

A bus driver needs
a cash tray for the
fares he collects,
an emergency
ticket pack,
a fare chart and
a module for the
bus's ticket machine.

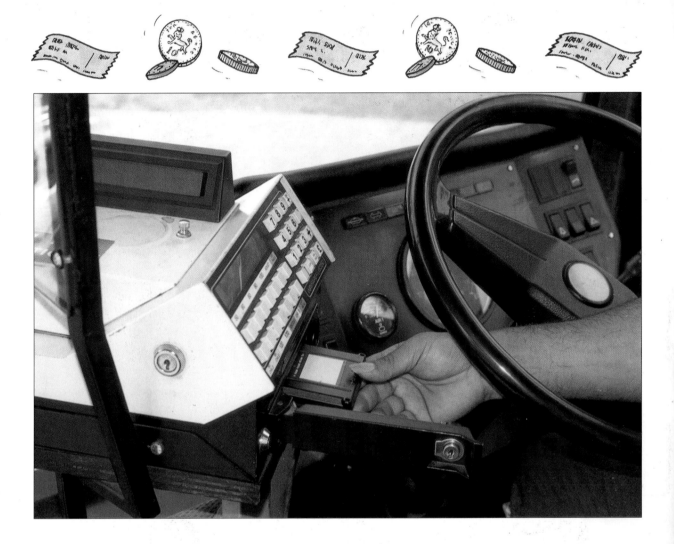

Winston slots his module
into the ticket machine on the bus.
This records all the fares that
he takes and adds up how much
money Winston has collected.

Next Winston sets the destination blind to show where the bus is going. Then he carries out a pre-start vehicle check.

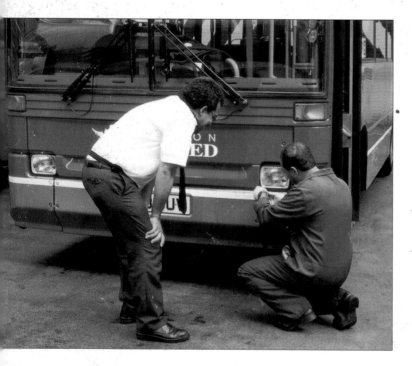

"This headlight needs changing," he tells John, the engineer. John fixes it straightaway.

Now Winston is ready
to set out on his route.

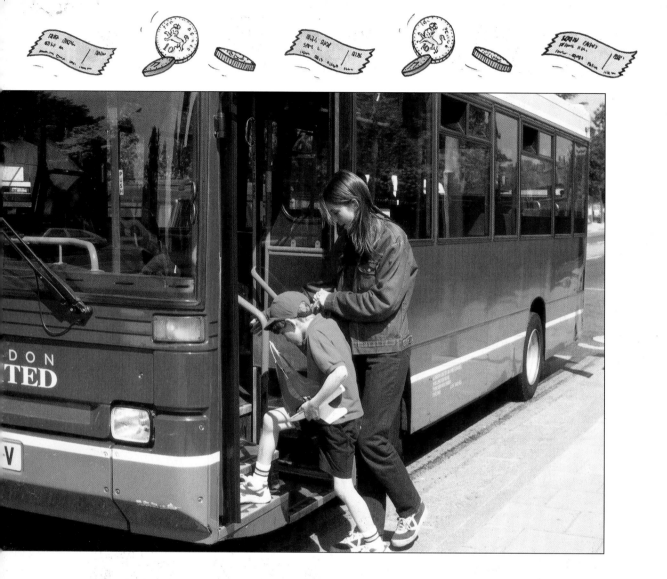

The bus stops for lots of passengers.
At one stop Ben and his sister Ellie
get on. "We're going to the park to sail
my boat," Ben tells Winston.

"That will be eighty pence," says Winston. He gives Ben and Ellie their tickets and change, and they find a seat.

Winston makes
more stops and
the bus starts to
fill up with passengers.

Mrs Murray is
struggling to lift
her shopping
on to the bus.

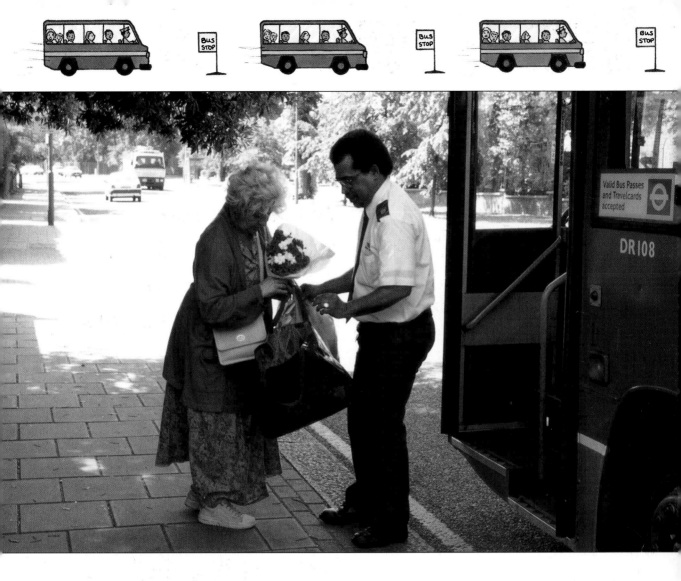

"Let me help you," says Winston.
He climbs out of his seat and
helps the lady with her bags.
"Thank you," says Mrs Murray.

The bus is quite crowded now and
there is nowhere for the lady to sit.
"Would you like my seat?" asks Ben.
He stands up so that Mrs Murray
can sit down.

"It's our stop next, Ellie," says Ben.
"I'll press the bell." The bell rings
to let Winston know that passengers
want him to stop.

Ben and Ellie climb off the bus, the door closes and Winston drives away.

"Oh no!" shouts Ben. "I've left my boat on the bus."

At the terminus Winston checks
the bus for lost property. "Oh dear,"
he says to himself, "the boy left his
boat behind. He will be upset."

Winston takes the boat to the
Lost Property Office at the garage.

Now it is time for his
meal break. In the
canteen Winston checks
over the route for the
other 'half' of his day.

Next Winston is going to drive
a different bus. He takes over
from Millie who has been driving
it all morning. "The traffic's not too
bad," she tells him.

At the end of his day Winston returns to the bus garage. A machine prints the amount of money he has collected and gives him a driver's receipt.

Winston puts the money in a counting machine.

He sees Ben at the
Lost Property Office.
"Thank you for
looking after my
boat," says Ben.

Winston smiles
and waves.
Then he sets
off for home.

Plan your own bus route

Make a plan of the bus route from your house to school, or your favourite shop. Mark on it all the bus stops that you pass along the way.

← my house

← Sam's house

shops ↓

- Who else lives along the route?
- Which shops do you pass?
- Is there a church, library or anything else of interest along the way?

church

swimming pool →

- How much is the fare from your house to school?

- What coins do you need to have for the exact fare?

- Find out the fares for other stops along the route.

- Mark them on your map.

Sally's house →

park

school

playing fields ↑

flats ←

How you can help bus drivers

1. Try to have the correct money ready before you get on the bus.

2. Don't put your feet on the seats.

3. Give up your seat if an elderly person or a pregnant woman has nowhere to sit.

4. Chat quietly to your friends – rowdy behaviour is a nuisance to the driver and the other passengers.

5. If you have a bus pass make sure the details are clearly visible.

6. Check you have all your belongings before you leave the bus.

7. If you know where you are going to get off, press the bell well before the stop.

Facts about bus drivers

- To be a bus driver you need to have a driving licence. Then you apply to the Recruitment Department of your local bus company.

- An instructor from the company tests new drivers' skills by watching how they drive in a van. If they are successful they take a written test and have an interview.

- If they pass these stages a doctor examines the new drivers to see if they are fit and well. Then they can begin training.

- After about 2-3 weeks, trainee bus drivers should be ready to take the Public Carriage Vehicle driving test. If they pass the test they are sent to the garage at which they will work.

- At that garage a new driver is trained to drive all the different kinds of buses and routes that are used there. Then the bus driver begins work.

- Winston, the bus driver in this book, works in a busy city. His day is made up of two 'halves'. In each half he makes four journeys. He is driving a pay-as-you-enter bus.

Index

© 1997 Franklin Watts

This edition 2001

Franklin Watts
96 Leonard Street
London EC2A 4XD

Franklin Watts Australia
56 O'Riordan Street
Alexandria, Sydney, NSW 2015

ISBN 0 7496 4101 0

Dewey Decimal Classification
Number 388.3

10 9 8 7 6 5 4 3

Editor: Sarah Ridley
Design: Kirstie Billingham
Photography: Harry Cory-Wright
Illustration: Kim Woolley

With thanks to Winston Jones
and his son, Millie Daniel, Joan
Murray-Brown, Ellie and Ben
Hodgson, Vic Hornblow, Ray
Loraine and London United
Busways Ltd.

A CIP catalogue record for this book
is available from the British Library.

Printed in Malaysia